Rising Higher

Spirituality and Grace in the Healing of Generational Dysfunction

STEPHANIE MURPHY

WESTBOW
PRESS®
A DIVISION OF THOMAS NELSON
& ZONDERVAN

WestBow Press books may be ordered through booksellers or by contacting:

WestBow Press
A Division of Thomas Nelson & Zondervan
1663 Liberty Drive
Bloomington, IN 47403
www.westbowpress.com
1 (866) 928-1240

ISBN: 978-1-9736-9035-1 (sc)
ISBN: 978-1-9736-9036-8 (hc)
ISBN: 978-1-9736-9034-4 (e)

Library of Congress Control Number: 2020907344

Print information available on the last page.

WestBow Press rev. date: 07/29/2020

To _____

From _____

*I dedicate this book to all who grew up in
dysfunction, became Christian believers, and
learned that through God's grace, the bonds of
generational dysfunction can be broken.*

But they that wait upon the Lord shall renew *their* strength; they shall mount up with wings as eagles; they shall run, and not be weary; *and* they shall walk and not faint.

—Isaiah 40:31 (KJV)

No, in all these things we are more than conquerors through him who loved us. For I am convinced that neither death nor life, neither angels nor demons, neither the present nor the future, nor any powers, neither height nor depth, nor anything else in all creation, will be able to separate us from the love of God that is in Christ Jesus our Lord.

—Romans 8:37–39 (NIV)

Contents

Introduction

Have you ever known someone who has had to overcome one obstacle after another just to get to a healthy place—a place that many others seem to arrive at naturally? Perhaps you're that person who has come a very long way from where you started, but it hasn't been easy. I am that person, and during my thirty years as a professional marriage and family therapist, I have counseled many individuals who have walked this path as well.

We are overcomers, conquerors! Through blood, sweat, and tears, we have risen above our generational dysfunctions. Well, hopefully not through blood, but for some that may have been the case. Some of us have broken dysfunctional patterns that date back many generations in our family histories. Others, like myself, have salvaged the healthy parts of our family heritage—parts that weren't always present in our childhood homes because of a parent's personal difficulties, such as depression, epilepsy, and other disabilities.

Professional psychotherapy has helped many people sort things out, bring their hurts to the surface, and learn to exonerate parents who were less than perfect. The field of family therapy held a natural attraction for me as a profession. As I studied family and relationship dynamics, I began to see the gaps in my upbringing—gaps that left me at a disadvantage as I tried to maneuver through young adulthood, marriage, and raising my own family.

Yet the strong desire to rise above these generational dysfunctions, to walk a different path, has always been a part of who I am. As a child, I remember being responsible beyond my years, studying hard and making good grades, cleaning the house without being told to do so, and disliking the laziness I saw all around me. I strived for excellence instead of mediocrity, for spirituality rather than faithlessness.

Many people allow themselves to become victims of their generational dysfunctions. They live out their days repeating the mistakes of their parents and grandparents, taking the path that is most familiar to them. They build multifaceted, impenetrable ego defenses that allow them to continue in their dysfunction. These defenses keep them from taking responsibility for their behaviors—since it is always someone else's fault!

I have found my personal relationship with Christ to be an integral part of my journey of faith through generational dysfunction. My heavenly Father has been faithful to reparent me in the areas where my parents fell short. The Holy Spirit leads me day by day as I continue to rise above self-defeating patterns, self-doubt, and insecurities. May you also find our heavenly Father to be a good, good Father as you trust in His love and grace. May His Word provide the light you need to illuminate your path as you find healing and overcome your generational dysfunctions.

But the mercy of the Lord is from everlasting to everlasting upon them that fear him, and His righteousness unto children's children.

—Psalm 103:17 (KJV)

1

Generational Dysfunction

As a professional therapist, I have always wondered how we reconcile generational dysfunction with living the Christian life. Maybe I've thought about this more than other people because I've spent so many years counseling Christians who were steeped in dysfunctional mind-sets and behaviors that were sabotaging their lives. And yes, all the while, I was coming to terms with my own generational issues.

Of course there is a connection between generational dysfunction and our sin nature. The battle goes on inside of us. Paul says in Romans 7:21–23 (NIV), "So I find this law at work: Although I want to do good, evil is right there with me. For in my inner being I delight in God's law; but I see another law at work in me, waging war against the law of my mind and making me a prisoner of the law of sin at work within me."

This scripture poses quite a dilemma for Christians, doesn't it? Many of the people I counseled wanted to be kind, yet their marriages were being destroyed by anger issues—behavioral patterns they had witnessed in a parent or grandparent. Others struggled with negative patterns of irrational fear and worry that had a crippling effect on their lives. Although they had read the Bible's teachings on peace and trust, they carried on the same thinking patterns that were familiar to them. Some would say, "We're just a family of worrywarts," without fully understanding the impact of their statement.

And then there is the age-old generational dysfunction of low self-esteem. The childhood tapes playing in their heads were louder than what God's Word had to say about who they are in Christ. These messages become stronger and more believable as they are passed down to children from parents who struggle with their own insecurities.

So what do we do? Are we truly "wretched," as Paul says in Romans 7:24 (NIV), or is there help? Verse 25 goes on to say, "Thanks be to God, who delivers me through Jesus Christ our Lord!" Paul then explains that we are not in the realm of the flesh but in the realm of the Spirit if the Spirit of God lives in us. If we walk in the Spirit, we will no longer be slaves to the desires of the flesh. Freedom! Freedom from generational dysfunction comes through Christ!

We are admonished in Philippians 2:5 (KJV), which says, "Let this mind be in you, which was also in Christ Jesus." As a believer, God has adopted you into His family. So why not let go of the dysfunctions you inherited from your earthly family and become more and more like your heavenly Father?

In my own family, I grew up with a mother who suffered from severe epilepsy and depression. Although she grew up in a stable, salt-of-the-earth family, life was immersed in dysfunction because of her disability. It affected the person she married and what she had to offer as a parent. As a child, I had the unique contrast of two very different settings. I spent every weekend at my maternal grandparents' home, basking in their love and adoration. During the week, I switched back over to practically raising myself in a family of stepsiblings. Although basic needs for food, clothing, and shelter were met, there was an emotional and spiritual barrenness.

My mother was gentle and kind, but she was emotionally remote due to her disabilities. I saw her as a victim of her circumstances, and early on, I remember feeling sorry for her. Trying to lighten her load, I became the parent, coming home from school to clean the house and launder clothes. This situation was not all bad. I have chosen to shake off the negative and hold on to the positive things I learned from my childhood.

My early experiences have made me very responsible and empathetic to others—traits that have served me well in my professional career. And I am grateful for the good fortune I had of having grandparents who were willing to fill in some of the gaps. My positive experiences with my grandparents have enabled me to have close relationships with my own grandchildren. On more than one occasion, when my grown children have observed me interacting with one of my grandchildren, they have said, "It's a beautiful thing to watch the two of you."

You see, if we choose to learn from the dysfunction of our parents rather than allow it to define who we are, we can rise above it with God's grace and make something good out of it. In other words, we can choose to see it as having purpose.

Reflections

1. Identify three areas of generational dysfunction in your family.

_____

_____

_____

_____

2. Which area seems to have the greatest stronghold in your life?

_____

_____

_____

_____

3. How has this generational dysfunction affected you personally?

_____

_____

_____

_____

4. How has this affected your relationships?

_____

_____

_____

_____

Journal Your Thoughts and Feelings

_____

_____

_____

_____

_____

_____

_____

_____

_____

_____

_____

_____

_____

_____

_____

_____

_____

_____

_____

_____

_____

_____

_____

_____

_____

_____

2

Our Dysfunction for His Grace

Our dysfunction for His grace! Isn't that how most of us come to God? There we are, standing before Him, reeking with the stench of our human failings and dysfunction. And how does He meet us? Is it with contempt or anger? No! Because of Christ, He extends His grace.

Can you picture the scene in your mind? A holy, righteous God is reaching out His hand of grace to us as we stand before Him disheveled, unkempt, and with all our generational dysfunctions in tow. We are saved by grace as we come to the feet of Jesus and ask Him to be our Savior.

He knows we can't clean up our act, at least not in our own power, so He offers us grace. His grace is sufficient for us because His strength is made perfect in our weaknesses.

Does He want us to continue in our dysfunctional way of life? Of course not! As believers, we are admonished in God's Word to become more and more like Christ. It is a lifelong process to grow in Christ. I'm grateful for God's patience with us, for His love and compassion for us, and for His grace!

Hebrews 5:15–16 (NIV) tells us, "For we do not have a high priest who is unable to empathize with our weaknesses, but we have one who has been tempted in every way, just as we are—yet he did not sin. Let us then approach God's throne of grace with confidence, so that we may receive mercy and find grace to help us in our time of need." You see, Jesus makes a trade with us. He took our sins upon Himself and gave us forgiveness and grace in return. Who would lay down His life for others? Who would leave the splendor of heaven to come down here and save us? Jesus did!

I am grateful for God's gift of eternal life, as John 3:16 (KJV) depicts: "For God so loved the world that He gave His only begotten Son, that whosoever believeth in Him should not perish but have everlasting life." His grace has made all the difference in the world in my life. It has been said that the Christian life is made up of many new beginnings. We may stumble and fall, yet it is in those times, when He is there to pick us up, that we experience the greatest spiritual growth.

Reflections

1. Describe when you first came to Christ.

_____

_____

_____

_____

2. How did you attempt to clean up your life before coming to Christ?

_____

_____

_____

_____

3. Describe a time when you stumbled and fell after your salvation.

_____

_____

_____

_____

4. What does God's grace look like to you?

_____

_____

_____

_____

Journal Your Thoughts and Feelings

_____

_____

_____

_____

_____

_____

_____

_____

_____

_____

_____

_____

_____

_____

_____

_____

_____

_____

_____

_____

_____

_____

_____

_____

So if the Son makes you free, you will be free indeed.
—John 8:36 (NASB)

3

My Chains Are Gone; I've Been Set Free

So you've come to Jesus, asked forgiveness for your sins, and accepted Him as your Savior. Here you are, standing before Him, with all your generational dysfunctions in tow. But God now sees you through Christ's righteousness—clean rather than tainted by sin and clothed, as it were, in a white robe instead of filthy rags.

As you look around, you can see the chains that had bound you to your sin and generational dysfunctions are gone—you've been set free! By faith, you can walk away and leave the rubble of your former life behind. You can walk in newness of life.

And many do just that, never looking back. Others walk away, but before they get too far, they glance back over their shoulders. Some never leave their baggage behind; instead, they pick it up and carry it along with them as they try to live the Christian life. You may ask, "Why in the world would they do that? They don't have to."

Maybe you are the one looking back over your shoulder, or the one laboring to carry those dysfunctions and imaginary chains with you. If so, can you visualize how different it looks for the believer who walks away from past bondage and begins walking with freedom in Christ?

Let's contrast the three examples. I picture those who walk in freedom from the weight of sin and dysfunction with a spring in their step and a smile on their faces as they eagerly embrace new life with trust and anticipation. Those who look back over their shoulders are tentative, are unsure of their decisions, and at times yearn for the familiarity of their old lives.

The Christians who hold on to the past are the most miserable. They move slowly and are bent over by the weight they carry. Their pasts are so much a part of who they are that they overshadow their identity in Christ. Life continues to be a struggle for them, and unfortunately at times, it is a struggle of their own making. They've forgotten that they are free.

May all of us, as Christians, remember who we are in Christ. And even though at times we think we feel their pull, may we render our generational dysfunctions powerless in the light of God's Word. Psalm 107:14 (NIV) tells us, "He brought them out of darkness, the utter darkness, and broke away their chains." John 8:36 (NIV) says, "So if the Son sets you free, you will be free indeed."

Many hold on to their pasts after becoming Christians. They struggle most of their lives under the weight of addictions, anger, or relationship issues. But they don't have to. You see, you come to a fork in the road when you encounter Christ. You can't straddle the two paths because the distance between them becomes too wide. At some point, you have to choose your path, or your path will choose you. May you have the courage to take the road that leads to wholeness and freedom from generational dysfunction—the path that leads to peace!

Reflections

1. What imaginary chains are holding you back in life?

   _____

   _____

   _____

   _____

2. Which of the three examples best describes you? Why?

   _____

   _____

   _____

   _____

3. When are you most likely to feel the pull of generational dysfunction?

   _____

   _____

   _____

   _____

   _____

4. Have you chosen your path, or has your path chosen you? In what way?

   _____

   _____

   _____

   _____

Journal Your Thoughts and Feelings

_____

_____

_____

_____

_____

_____

_____

_____

_____

_____

_____

_____

_____

_____

_____

_____

_____

_____

_____

_____

_____

_____

_____

_____

_____

4

God Did Not Forget about You

My husband and I recently went to see the movie about Steve McQueen's life, as documented by Greg Laurie. I came away moved by what I saw—a loving, heavenly Father reaching out His hand to a man who grew up without love. Steve had acted out his family's unresolved generational dysfunctions for most of his life—until God allowed him to cross paths with an older Christian man. This flight instructor took him under his wing and showed him God's love.

The movie proceeded to tell how Steve started going to church with his friend. During one of the services, he accepted Christ as his personal Savior, and he later had a private conversation with the pastor to solidify his decision. After becoming terminally ill, Steve talked about his regrets of not having more time to tell people about what Jesus had done for him. I thought it was so good that Greg Laurie was now telling his story for him.

You see, God did not forget about Steve McQueen, and

He did not forget about you. He looks through our veneer, our defenses, and sees the soft hearts of wounded children. God sees the hurt and the longing for love. And yes, He sees the dysfunction and sin—but He meets us where we are, with His grace.

The movie talked about Billy Graham meeting Steve on the airplane that was flying him to Mexico for medical treatment. He came and talked and prayed with Steve. As Billy Graham was leaving, Steve's last words to him were, "I'll see you in heaven." And he will because God did not forget about Steve McQueen!

If you are living your life as a reaction to your family's generational issues—maybe intense anger or hurt—I encourage you to find peace and love in the arms of your heavenly Father. You don't have to live your life feeling unloved or neglected. God offers to be a Father to the fatherless, as Psalm 68:5 (NIV) tells us: "A father to the fatherless, is God in His holy dwelling."

If your parents weren't able to give you the love you needed as a child, you might have inadvertently closed up your heart to protect yourself from further hurt. In doing so, you have also chosen a path of loneliness and lack of intimacy. I want to encourage you to open your heart to God and allow Him to heal your hurts. Only then will you be whole enough to risk opening your heart to others.

Reflections

1. Is there anyone in your life who shows you what God's love looks like? Who?

_____

_____

_____

_____

2. Have you ever felt that God has forgotten about you? If so, in what way?

_____

_____

_____

_____

3. Describe how you view your heavenly Father. Is your perspective affected by the way you were treated by your earthly father, grandfather, or other father figure?

_____

_____

_____

_____

4. What can you do today to open your heart to others?

_____

_____

_____

Journal Your Thoughts and Feelings

_____

_____

_____

_____

_____

_____

_____

_____

_____

_____

_____

_____

_____

_____

_____

_____

_____

_____

_____

_____

_____

_____

_____

_____

_____

_____

_____

_____

See what great love the Father has lavished on us, that we should be called children of God! And that is what we are!

—1 John 3:1 (NIV)

5

Know You Are His Child

Until you know in your heart of hearts—not just in your head—that through Christ, you have been adopted into God's family, you will have difficulty letting go of your past. Yes, you will always be the offspring of your earthly parents, and if they are Christians and are living godly lives, their examples will help you realize your identity in Christ.

What if your parents aren't Christians, or what if you have Christian parents who still struggle with their generational issues? If this is the case, you will have to look deeply into God's Word to fully understand how God has accepted you into His family. If you did not feel loved by your parents, it would be difficult for you to comprehend His love for you.

The examples of other committed believers will help you as well. You will then learn to base your perspective about life and about yourself on God's Word—not on the old messages you heard growing up. In other words, you stop believing the lies.

You will have to adapt to being adopted into God's

family and learn to embrace all that means, rather than continuing to believe that your earthly heritage is your lot in life. Developing a new identity in Christ and understanding that being a child of God means you are valued and loved by your heavenly Father is a great heritage.

John 1:12 (NASB) tells us, "But as many as received Him, to them He gave the right to become children of God, even to those who believe in His name." Romans 8:14–16 (NIV) says, "For those who are led by the Spirit of God are the children of God. The Spirit you received does not make you slaves so that you live in fear again; rather, the Spirit you received brought about your adoption to sonship. And by Him we cry, *'Abba*, Father. The Spirit himself testifies with our spirit that we are God's children.'"

May you find your true identity as a child of God and discover the love, joy, and peace that are now your heritage.

Reflections

1. In what ways do you feel loved by your family? In what ways do you feel unloved?

_____

_____

_____

_____

2. What is the most critical generational issue that your parents have not resolved?

_____

_____

_____

_____

3. In what way is your identity in Christ different from the sense of identity you developed in your family of origin?

_____

_____

_____

_____

4. What do you think the Bible teaches about being a part of the family of God?

_____

_____

_____

_____

Journal Your Thoughts and Feelings

_____

_____

_____

_____

_____

_____

_____

_____

_____

_____

_____

_____

_____

_____

_____

_____

_____

_____

_____

_____

_____

_____

_____

_____

_____

_____

_____

_____

_____

_____

6

By the Spirit

God's Word tells us that it is by the Spirit that we rise above sin and our old behaviors and thinking patterns. Our mind-sets shift from being focused on what we want to what the Spirit desires. This transformation leads to life and peace. Romans 8:5–6 (NIV) says, "Those who live according to the flesh have their minds set on what the flesh desires; but those who live in accordance with the Spirit have their minds set on what the Spirit desires. The mind governed by the Spirit is life and peace."

It is easy to walk in the flesh—anyone can do it. It is a self-pleasing path, full of selfish ambition and self-absorption. It often moves us quickly along as we chase after various things that we think will make us happy—wealth, good looks, and recognition, to name a few. As we hurry on our way, we often miss the small pleasures of life—a magnificent sunset, a purposeful conversation with a friend, or time playing on the floor with our child or grandchild.

If we're not careful, we can miss seeing into another's heart, seeing someone's hurt and pain—missing the opportunity to show empathy. Although our chosen path seems to make us happy, it is only for a season. Selfish endeavors do not nurture our spiritual and emotional growth. Instead, selfishness stagnates our growth.

In contrast, when we are led by the Holy Spirit, filled with the Spirit, and walk in the Spirit, our lives are different. We aren't trying to live in our own strength, nor do we depend solely on our knowledge or resources. Instead, day by day, we are learning to rely on the power, wisdom, and comfort of the Holy Spirit. God knew what we needed to live victorious Christian lives in this world, and He made provision for us by giving us His Holy Spirit to indwell us. This gift is a mystery to those who have not had their spiritual eyes opened, yet it is a beautiful truth to those who follow Christ!

Reflections

1. What is your understanding of what it means to live in accordance with the Spirit?

_____

_____

_____

_____

2. How difficult is it for you to focus on what the Spirit wants instead of what the flesh wants?

_____

_____

_____

_____

3. Give an example of one way you can rely on the power, wisdom, and comfort of the Holy Spirit rather than depending solely on your own resources.

_____

_____

_____

_____

4. In what way has a spiritual mind-set helped you to rise above generational dysfunction in your life?

_____

_____

_____

Journal Your Thoughts and Feelings

_____

_____

_____

_____

_____

_____

_____

_____

_____

_____

_____

_____

_____

_____

_____

_____

_____

_____

_____

_____

_____

_____

_____

_____

_____

_____

_____

_____

7

Foreigners

When we accept Christ's sacrifice for our sins, we are redeemed from the old way of living that we inherited from our earthly families. First Peter 1:17–19 (NIV) admonishes us, "Since you call on a Father who judges each person's work impartially, live out your time as foreigners here in reverent fear. For you know that it was not with perishable things such as silver or gold that you were redeemed from the empty way of life handed down to you from your ancestors, but with the precious blood of Christ, a lamb without blemish or defect." Yes, we are to live as foreigners. That which was familiar to us now becomes foreign—the angry response, the fear, selfishness, or immorality.

1 Peter 1:14–16 (NIV) speaks of a new way of life: "As obedient children, do not conform to the evil desires you had when you lived in ignorance. But just as he who called you is holy, so be holy in all you do; for it is written: 'Be holy, because I am holy.' " Wow! A high standard for us! Something very

foreign to us, and yet Peter states it clearly. That doesn't sound like we are to go on living out our generational dysfunction. Still, some struggle with letting go of familiar mind-sets and behaviors. They've forgotten that their lives are redeemed, that they are born again. "For you have been born again, not of perishable seed, but of imperishable, through the living and enduring word of God." (1 Peter 1:23 NIV).

Learning to live as a foreigner on this earth is an essential part of breaking free of the strongholds that are sabotaging your life. You will experience God's grace and love as He empowers you to live as His child. May God bless you as you become more Christlike and as you realize that your life on this earth is preparation for eternity in heaven.

Reflections

1. What generational patterns have you held on to simply because they are familiar?

   _____

   _____

   _____

   _____

2. What is the most challenging thing you have changed in your life since becoming a follower of Christ?

   _____

   _____

   _____

   _____

3. List three healthy patterns handed down to you from your parents or grandparents.

   _____

   _____

   _____

   _____

4. In what ways do you view your life on earth as a preparation for eternity?

   _____

   _____

   _____

   _____

Journal Your Thoughts and Feelings

_____

_____

_____

_____

_____

_____

_____

_____

_____

_____

_____

_____

_____

_____

_____

_____

_____

_____

_____

_____

_____

_____

_____

_____

_____

_____

_____

Happy *is* the man *that* findeth wisdom, and the man *that* getteth understanding. For the merchandise of it *is* better than the merchandise of silver and the gain thereof than fine gold.

—Proverbs 3:13–14 (KJV)

8

Wisdom Instead of Dysfunction

When people repeatedly dump their negativity onto others, they have learned a very dysfunctional coping mechanism. Have you ever noticed that afterward, the person seems to feel better, whereas the one dumped on is left to clean up the mess? That's not fair!

Let's say these people have some legitimate stress in their lives, as we all do. However, by the time we are adults, most of us have developed healthy coping mechanisms that allow us to process stress in ways that are not harmful to ourselves or others. We are, for the most part, living healthy, functional lives. We process our feelings, think rational thoughts, problem-solve, and move forward through the ups and downs of life. We understand that once we accept the difficulties of life, we can transcend or rise above those difficulties.

We have learned to take responsibility for our own lives and actions. This level of maturity frees us from the dysfunctional pattern of blaming others for our difficulties or unhappiness. We don't victimize people with our anger or frustration. Instead, we own it. In other words, we tell ourselves, "This is my problem. I'm the one having difficulty here. Therefore, it is my responsibility to either find a solution or accept what I cannot change. Dumping my negative feelings all over another person is not an option. I can respectfully assert myself and ask for change, but I do not demand, intimidate, or manipulate."

Most of us learn to be happy about the success of others. We build them up and don't need to tear them down or level the playing field. We are aware of our strengths and weaknesses and accept our worth. It is not necessary to view ourselves as better than others to feel good about ourselves. Instead, we can cheer them on, compliment them, and see their potential. We don't pick others apart or gossip about them as a way of making ourselves look or feel superior.

Proverbs 4:7 (KJV) tells us, "Wisdom is the principal thing; therefore get wisdom: and with all thy getting get understanding." If you have learned dysfunctional coping mechanisms that are wreaking havoc on your relationships, I want to encourage you to choose the path that leads to wisdom.

Reflections

1. In what way are you allowing negative people to affect your life?

_____

_____

_____

_____

2. What healthy coping mechanisms have you developed at this stage of your life? What unhealthy coping mechanisms have you developed?

_____

_____

_____

_____

3. Are any of your negative behaviors affecting others?

_____

_____

_____

_____

4. What steps can you take today to take more responsibility for your life, your behavior, and your relationships?

_____

_____

_____

_____

Journal Your Thoughts and Feelings

_____

_____

_____

_____

_____

_____

_____

_____

_____

_____

_____

_____

_____

_____

_____

_____

_____

_____

_____

_____

_____

_____

_____

_____

_____

_____

_____

9

Kindness Rather Than Criticism

Some people grow up around criticism and judgment, to the point that it becomes second nature to them. They don't think twice about ripping apart another person's character. It is very dysfunctional for Christians to use their words in this manner.

Everyone seems to have an opinion these days, and people think it is their God-given purpose in life to air that opinion. But we end up sounding foolish and do the work of God a disservice when we use our perspective as an excuse for unkindness and character assassination. None of us has enough information to stand in judgment of another person. Only God does.

What matters is what God says about the way we treat one another. Let's take a look at some scriptures that speak to this issue.

> "And be ye kind one to another, tenderhearted, forgiving one another, even as God for Christ's sake hath forgiven you." (Ephesians 4:32 KJV)

"And walk in love, as Christ also hath loved us, and hath given himself for us an offering and a sacrifice to God for a sweetsmelling savour." (Ephesians 5:2 KJV)

"Who are you to judge the servant of another? To his own master he stands or falls; and he will stand, for the Lord is able to make him stand." (Romans 14:4 NASB)

"You then, why do you judge your brother or sister? Or why do you treat them with contempt? For we will all stand before God's judgment seat." (Romans 14:10 NIV)

"Do not judge, or you too will be judged. For in the same way you judge others, you will be judged, and with the measure you use it will be measured to you. Why do you look at the speck of sawdust in your brother's eye and pay no attention to the plank in your own eye?" (Matthew 7:1–3 NIV)

"Accept one another, then, just as Christ accepted you, in order to bring praise to God." (Romans 15:7 NIV)

May each of us choose kindness rather than criticism.

Reflections

1. What role models do you have for kindness?

_____

_____

_____

_____

2. Is there anything you would like to change about the way you treat other people?

_____

_____

_____

_____

3. How would you describe Christ's example when it comes to kindness?

_____

_____

_____

_____

4. Are you able to empathize with someone who is being treated unkindly? In what way?

_____

_____

_____

_____

Journal Your Thoughts and Feelings

_____

_____

_____

_____

_____

_____

_____

_____

_____

_____

_____

_____

_____

_____

_____

_____

_____

_____

_____

_____

_____

_____

_____

_____

_____

Like a city whose walls are broken through is a person who lacks self-control.

—Proverbs 25:28 (NIV)

10

Stability Rather Than Reactivity

Emotional reactivity is one of the most prevalent indicators of emotional dysfunction. By this, I mean a person reacts to a situation instead of choosing his or her actions or words. In family therapy, we call it being undifferentiated from one's family of origin. For example, you may have seen the cartoon of the adult coming home for a visit with parents. The adult gets smaller and smaller the closer he approaches his parents' front door and then becomes a child when he is greeted at the door by a parent.

Many people never learn to establish a healthy sense of self around their parents. This lack of differentiation usually results from the parents not being well differentiated in their own family of origin. Therefore, they pass this way of interacting down to their children. Boundaries are crossed time and again as children grow up, and they never learn to think for themselves because they are either trying to please their parents or spending their lives reacting in anger or resentment toward their parents. This reactivity carries over to all areas of life—work, marriage, parenting, and friendships.

It requires some concentrated effort, usually with the help of a professional therapist, to break this pattern. I coach my patients to have short visits in which they can begin relating to their parents, adult to adult, without getting sucked into the old ways of interacting. And believe me, the more a person works on differentiating, the harder the parent or another person will try to pull him or her back into the original pattern. It's like a washing machine being off balance. When the dynamics change, the natural pull is for the other person to attempt to bring back what he or she perceives as balance, regardless of how unhealthy it is. You see, the tendency for all of us is to gravitate toward what is familiar; in therapy, we call it homeostasis.

Romans 12:17–18 (ESV) tells us, "Repay no one evil for evil, but give thought to do what is honorable in the sight of all. If possible, so far as it depends on you, live peaceably with all." In other words, don't be reactive! Instead, give thought to how you respond to people and circumstances. Only then will you be able to have stability in your relationships and your life. You won't be driven about with every passing wind, bouncing around from one relationship to another or one job after another. Instead, you will reap the benefits found in steadiness: lasting relationships, deep connections, and the success that only comes from perseverance.

Reflections

1. On a scale of one to ten, how differentiated are you from your parents?

_____

_____

_____

_____

2. Do you feel that your parents respect your boundaries as an adult child? If not, in what ways are those boundaries violated?

_____

_____

_____

_____

3. How were boundaries respected (or crossed) in your childhood home?

_____

_____

_____

_____

4. How do your parents react or respond when you set boundaries with them?

_____

_____

_____

Journal Your Thoughts and Feelings

_____

_____

_____

_____

_____

_____

_____

_____

_____

_____

_____

_____

_____

_____

_____

_____

_____

_____

_____

_____

_____

_____

_____

_____

_____

_____

_____

11

Parental Loyalty

Most of us think of parental loyalty as a good thing, and it is—within reason. It can also be distorted into an unhealthy sense of obligation, guilt, and need to please. When an adult child gives a parent's words too much power, it affects every aspect of that person's life—decisions, life choices, relationships, self-esteem, and boundaries.

A young divorced mother of two reports acute anxiety upon entering therapy. She cites a stressful work environment as the trigger for her increased stress levels. Yet upon further exploration, it is evident that the issue runs far deeper—it is generational. The dynamics of this young woman's work relationships resemble the type of relationship dynamic she has with her mother. She feels emotionally exploited, controlled, and devalued. Her life feels chaotic as she struggles with decision-making and setting boundaries in relationships. She doubts herself at every turn and has allowed herself to become financially and emotionally dependent on her mother. As a result, she feels obligated to please and to follow unsolicited controlling advice.

She is confused as to why she is mistreated at work and in relationships with men. After all, "I'm a nice person," she says. Unfortunately, this otherwise positive attribute is doing her a disservice because of an exaggerated sense of parental loyalty. After being "too nice" to assert herself with her mother, she has also been "too nice" to stand up for herself in her marriage or at work. She has allowed her kindness to be taken advantage of, and she is beginning to see the toll this is taking on her health, emotional well-being, and relationships. It has become more uncomfortable *not* to change than it is to change.

As a therapist, I want to help her learn to set healthy boundaries and to break the dysfunctional relationship pattern between herself and her mother. Then, I want her to become comfortable transferring these changes into other areas of her life. This transition may sound easy, but it will prove to be one of the most challenging things she has ever had to do in her life—because of an irrational sense of parental loyalty.

The key is to foster a healthy sense of adult autonomy while staying respectfully and lovingly connected to her mother. To accomplish this, she has to learn to assert herself as an adult in her own right. It will take time and many attempts at experimenting with and changing the family's unwritten terms of endearment. The goal is to build a healthy relationship between parent and adult child while simultaneously preserving the dignity and autonomy of both.

May we follow Jesus's command to "honor your father and mother" (Matthew 19:19 NIV) by learning to speak the truth in love as we kindly set healthy boundaries in our relationships.

Reflections

1. How would you describe healthy parental loyalty?

_____

_____

_____

_____

2. In what ways have you experienced an unhealthy sense of parental loyalty?

_____

_____

_____

_____

3. What boundaries do you need to set to break a dysfunctional relationship dynamic between yourself and your parents?

_____

_____

_____

_____

4. What steps can you take today to strengthen your sense of adult autonomy while staying connected to your family in a healthy way?

_____

_____

_____

_____

Journal Your Thoughts and Feelings

_____

_____

_____

_____

_____

_____

_____

_____

_____

_____

_____

_____

_____

_____

_____

_____

_____

_____

_____

_____

_____

_____

_____

_____

_____

_____

Be completely humble and gentle; be patient, bearing with one another in love.

—Ephesians 4:2 (NIV)

12

Is Generational Dysfunction Sabotaging Your Marriage?

If you are having difficulty in your marriage relationship and desire change, an excellent place to start is with your family history. I know this sounds like something your medical doctor would ask, but it also applies to relationship styles and patterns. When a couple comes to see me for marriage counseling, one of the first things I ask them to do is to complete a genogram. Similar to a family tree, the genogram looks back a few generations. The partners fill in as much information as they can about their parents, grandparents, and great-grandparents. In therapy, we are looking for patterns: divorce, alcoholism, anger issues, addictions, depression, anxiety, abuse, and so on.

Light bulbs come on as people look at their family dynamics diagrammed on a genogram. They can see the generational patterns and identify with the ones passed down to them—in other words, the ones their parents or grandparents didn't resolve in their lifetimes. You see, that's how it works. We pass the issues that we don't overcome in our lives down to our children. They can either resolve the issue and stop the generational pattern, or they continue to pass it down to their children. That's how generational dysfunction is perpetuated, often gaining momentum and strengthening as it goes from one generation to the next. This dynamic can be a good thing when it involves positive traits, such as kindness or helping others, but it is quite the opposite in situations like alcoholism or abuse.

Anger issues are a common reason couples seek marriage therapy. One spouse usually has an anger issue, and the other partner portrays the complimentary pattern of being codependent and unassertive. It becomes one of the perfect storms in marital therapy. Each partner brings his or her own generational issues into the marriage, with each person's role being a contributor to the couple's relational difficulties. Often, the person with the anger issue is singled out and identified as the patient, and the partner is allowed to take a victim role. The use of a genogram helps them see the problem as a relationship issue—one to which each person uniquely contributes. Only then will progress be made in therapy, as each person takes responsibility for his or her behaviors and attitudes and begins to work on changing oneself rather than focusing on changing the other.

Your marriage relationship will become healthier and more satisfying as you begin to change patterns that often feel familiar to you. You will experience the freedom that comes from choosing your behaviors, rather than emotionally reacting to situations. Ephesians 5:33 (NIV) gives us an example of what a healthy marriage looks like: "However, each one of you also must love his wife as he loves himself, and the wife must respect her husband." Remind yourself often that you can choose the scriptural model of marriage even if you have not seen it modeled by your parents.

Reflections

1. Have you ever made a genogram? If not, I encourage you to draw a simple genogram on a separate sheet of paper.

_____

_____

_____

_____

2. What generational patterns did you discover when you completed a family genogram?

_____

_____

_____

_____

3. What attitudes about marriage have been passed down to you by your parents or grandparents?

_____

_____

_____

_____

4. Are any of those attitudes sabotaging your marriage?

_____

_____

_____

_____

Journal Your Thoughts and Feelings

_____

_____

_____

_____

_____

_____

_____

_____

_____

_____

_____

_____

_____

_____

_____

_____

_____

_____

_____

_____

_____

_____

_____

_____

_____

_____

_____

_____

13

Homeostasis

Homeostasis is the pull to keep things the same. It is a systemic term that relates to how the body maintains its equilibrium. It adjusts to temperatures to maintain constant body temperature. Other systems also tend toward homeostasis—groups, families, societies. It's our human nature to resist change until it becomes more uncomfortable not to change than it is to change.

When clients walk through my door, I know they are there for one of two reasons. Either a spouse or other family member has demanded they begin therapy, or it has become more uncomfortable not to change than it is to change. In marriage, if a spouse is unassertive and goes along to get along, it is rare for the other spouse to initiate therapy. In most instances, the enabling spouse seeks treatment because he or she has become symptomatic—depressed, anxious, or indecisive.

In these situations, the solution has become a part of the problem. By desperately trying to keep things the same (possibly as they were in the early stages of the marriage or as the person has idealized), self-esteem and individuality are compromised. The unassertive spouse comes from a position of dependence rather than inner strength and interdependence.

When relationships and marriages become off balance due to one person's personal or spiritual growth, there will be a pull toward homeostasis. It doesn't matter if that pull is toward the familiar dysfunctional way of relating with each other; it is still there. That is why when one spouse comes to therapy alone, the chances of that couple divorcing are higher. As a marriage counselor, it is my ethical duty to advise a client of this dynamic. It doesn't mean the person should not seek therapy. People may have become so symptomatic as a result of relational stress that it is necessary to seek treatment.

You've heard the saying "It may get worse before it gets better." In relationships, because of the natural pull toward homeostasis, it usually does get worse before it gets better. If one spouse stops playing the game or changes the rhythm of their dysfunctional dance, the other one will try to return to what is familiar. If one stops reacting to the other's bad behavior, the partner may miss the emotional intensity and work even harder to evoke a negative reaction. This dynamic is especially relevant when one partner seeks a negative response from the other to feel superior or self-righteous.

As couples begin to learn healthier ways of relating to each other, over time they will create a new normal. When this happens, instead of being a negative dynamic, homeostasis takes on the new role of protecting and stabilizing healthy behaviors and positive relationship dynamics. As Christians, God's Word calls us to be stable in all our ways. "Therefore, my beloved brethren, be steadfast, immovable, always abounding in the work of the Lord." (1 Corinthians 15:58 NASB).

Reflections

1. What is homeostasis?

   _____

   _____

   _____

   _____

2. Describe a time when your marriage or relationship felt unbalanced.

   _____

   _____

   _____

   _____

3. Describe the pull of homeostasis in your family of origin.

   _____

   _____

   _____

   _____

4. What healthy relationship dynamics would you like to become your new normal?

   _____

   _____

   _____

   _____

   _____

Journal Your Thoughts and Feelings

_____

_____

_____

_____

_____

_____

_____

_____

_____

_____

_____

_____

_____

_____

_____

_____

_____

_____

_____

_____

_____

_____

_____

_____

_____

_____

_____

_____

14

Triggers

Have you ever had people defend their bad treatment of you on the premise that your behavior or words triggered them? We call this a cop-out. If they can blame you, they no longer have to feel guilty or responsible for their inappropriate behavior. I often tell my patients that this is the very reason that at, say, age sixty-five or even seventy-five, they are still dealing with behavior patterns that should have been long outgrown or discarded. Their defenses act as just that, defenses, defending their ego to the point that they are not accurately self-reflective.

Most of us have reached a healthy state of being and can self-reflect. That is, we can honestly assess our behavior and see when we are at fault. A feeling of guilt is healthy when it leads us to change those behaviors, ask forgiveness, and move forward without demolishing our sense of worth. We learn, and we grow from our mistakes rather than rationalizing them away and then repeating the same mistakes over and over. Somehow it is no longer a mistake but a purposeful refusal to accept responsibility for our behavior.

Our relationships can grow rather than stagnate, deteriorate, or disintegrate, but only when we accept responsibility for our part in those relationships. No self-respecting person will tolerate being someone else's whipping post indefinitely. People may hold on for a while, trying to understand the other person or even to evaluate their own behavior to see if they are at fault. Over time, as they realize it's not about them, they kick into self-preservation mode. If their attempts at confronting and asking for change continue to meet resistance, they will eventually pull back or remove themselves from the relationship.

Proverbs 22:24–25 (KJV) admonishes us, "Make no friendship with an angry man; and with a furious man thou shalt not go: Lest thou learn his ways and get a snare to thy soul." Sometimes, getting to a healthy place in our own lives will require us to make the difficult decision to remove ourselves from the path of an angry person who continues to point to triggers as his or her excuse for hostile, abusive behavior.

Reflections

1. Have you felt like a victim in a relationship where someone blamed you for triggering his or her anger? If so, in what way?

_____

_____

_____

_____

2. Do you have a habit of blaming others for your inappropriate behaviors? If so, in what way?

_____

_____

_____

_____

3. What steps can you take to become more self-reflecting?

_____

_____

_____

_____

4. Are there any current friendships in your life that you need to reevaluate in light of Proverbs 22:24–25?

_____

_____

_____

_____

Journal Your Thoughts and Feelings

_____

_____

_____

_____

_____

_____

_____

_____

_____

_____

_____

_____

_____

_____

_____

_____

_____

_____

_____

_____

_____

_____

_____

_____

_____

_____

_____

_____

_____

Brothers, do not be children in your thinking. Be infants in evil, but in your thinking be mature.

—1 Corinthians 14:20 (ESV)

15

Rising above Immaturity

How old are you? Twenty-five, or maybe sixty-five? It doesn't matter. Whatever your age, remember that babies don't grow up overnight, and neither will you. 1 Peter 2:1–3 (NIV) says, "Therefore, rid yourselves of all malice and all deceit, hypocrisy, envy, and slander of every kind. Like newborn babies, crave pure spiritual milk, so that by it you may grow up in your salvation, now that you have tasted that the Lord is good." This verse admonishes us to "crave pure spiritual milk." You may wonder what this means. Just as babies can't eat steak, we have to start with the easily digestible parts of God's Word as we grow up in Christ. We have to truly understand our salvation before we can grasp other, more in-depth topics, such as end-time events in the book of Revelation. For example, new Christians read the book of John and the gospels to solidify their faith.

It isn't easy for a person steeped in generational dysfunction to accurately reflect his or her biological age in terms of maturity level. I have counseled numerous individuals who were successful and accomplished in their careers or ministries. It was evident that they were intelligent human beings who could maneuver through life on a certain level—until they faced an emotionally challenging stressor or intimate relationship. Then things began to fall apart.

If you are dancing between stability and emotional unsteadiness, you are most likely dealing with patterns of thought and behavior that go back several generations in your family. God's Word is rich in wisdom and is full of examples to guide us in changing our unproductive ways. We have to know what healthy behaviors look like before we can abandon our familiar unhealthy ones. If this was not role-modeled for you by your parents, you have to start somewhere, no matter how old you are. I encourage you to begin taking steps in the right direction, even if they feel like baby steps. God will meet you right where you are as you grow in grace, knowledge, and maturity.

Reflections

1. In what ways are you satisfied with your maturity level?

_____

_____

_____

_____

2. In what areas of your life would you like to experience personal growth?

_____

_____

_____

_____

3. Is there a discrepancy in maturity level in some areas of your life? If so, where is the variance?

_____

_____

_____

_____

_____

4. What generational issues have affected your maturity?

_____

_____

_____

_____

Journal Your Thoughts and Feelings

_____

_____

_____

_____

_____

_____

_____

_____

_____

_____

_____

_____

_____

_____

_____

_____

_____

_____

_____

_____

_____

_____

_____

_____

_____

_____

_____

_____

_____

_____

16

Rising above Hurt

Perhaps you are walking around wounded. Other people may not even notice, but you still feel the sting. It could have been a parent's abuse or neglect during childhood that left you with painful emotional scars. Or maybe it was poverty, being bullied, or witnessing uncontrolled anger and violence in your home. Whatever the origin of your woundedness, it has taken a toll on you over the years. You may have become the one wounding others as you react to your own inner turmoil, or the victim who continues to surround yourself with people who use, drain, and devalue you.

If you find yourself in such a situation, I want to encourage you not to underestimate yourself. Don't believe the lies about your worth and potential. I want you to realize that the behavior of others toward you is not about you, but about them—often stemming from their own woundedness and generational dysfunction.

Once you break through denial and accept that you have been wounded by another person—usually by someone who is supposed to love, accept, and protect you—then you can begin the process of healing. As you learn to exonerate parents or others, you will be able to rid yourself of the heavy burdens of bitterness and unforgiveness that only serve the purpose of keeping your wounds open. As you begin to allow God's healing love to flow over you, your festering wounds are cleansed and your heart begins to heal.

Psalm 147:3 (NASB) tells us, "He heals the brokenhearted and binds up their wounds." God is faithful to do His part. As we release bitterness and unforgiveness, we allow space for His healing love to flow into our wounded hearts and make us whole again.

Reflections

1. Have you been wounded? If so, in what ways? By whom?

    _____

    _____

    _____

    _____

2. Are you harboring any bitterness as a result of being
    wounded?

    _____

    _____

    _____

    _____

3. In what ways have you hurt others as a reaction to your
    own hurt?

    _____

    _____

    _____

    _____

4. What steps can you begin taking to exonerate those who
    have hurt you and start allowing God's healing love to
    make you whole?

    _____

    _____

    _____

    _____

Journal Your Thoughts and Feelings

17

Regaining Your Equilibrium

How do you regain your equilibrium after being unexpectedly immersed in a family of origin issue—perhaps a wedding, a funeral, or graduation? Whatever the occasion, you are once again in close proximity with family members who trigger emotions and feelings you thought were deeply buried or healed. Maybe it is your father's funeral, and you are overwhelmed with sadness at the realization that your relationship issues will remain unresolved.

You discover that you're not quite the same when you return home to your normal environment and routines. Somehow, something is off. Your spouse says you are moody or distracted. Guilt seems to have attached itself to you like glue. You can't shake it. Realizing something is wrong, you may try to talk out your feelings with a trusted friend or a counselor.

When this scenario presents itself in my office, I first try to help my clients make the connection between their current feelings and the recent events. I want them to make this connection to be able to regain their equilibrium. The contact with extended family brought them face-to-face, again, with the dysfunction they had walked away from long ago. After thinking they had buffered themselves sufficiently, they are now alarmed at how raw and vulnerable they feel.

Once you make the connection, you are then able to work on shifting your focus back to your own life, to your own family, and to your strengths and blessings. The key is not to stay in a state of disequilibrium. You don't have to. Although the effects on your emotional state are real, they no longer have to have power over you. As you realize just how far you have come, how strong you are, and that you get to *choose* a healthy path, you begin to feel your personal power return. You are an adult, not a victim! You are independent, not dependent! And you are loved and valuable!

As Christians, we can draw upon the strength of our identity in Christ—to see ourselves as God sees us. We are who He says we are. We don't have to believe the old tapes from childhood. We can draw strength from the love of a heavenly Father who loves and enjoys us so much that He sings over us. As Zephaniah 3:17 (NIV) says, "The Lord your God is with you, the Mighty Warrior who saves. He will take great delight in you; in his love he will no longer rebuke you, but will rejoice over you with singing."

Reflections

1. Discuss a time when you felt you had to regain your equilibrium after being in a situation that triggered an old family of origin issue.

_____

_____

_____

_____

2. How did you know that something was off or out of balance afterward?

_____

_____

_____

_____

3. In what ways did you make the connection between your feelings and the events?

_____

_____

_____

_____

4. After making the connection, how difficult was it for you to shift your focus back to the positive things in your life?

_____

_____

_____

Journal Your Thoughts and Feelings

_____
_____
_____
_____
_____
_____
_____
_____
_____
_____
_____
_____
_____
_____
_____
_____
_____
_____
_____
_____
_____
_____
_____
_____
_____
_____
_____
_____

Cast all your anxiety on him because he cares for you.

—1 Peter 5:7 (NIV)

18

Rising above Guilt

I have worked with people who have come so far, and yet at times they seem to be carrying a sense of guilt for things that are not their responsibility. Family members can take all kinds of directions in life. Some may rise above the dysfunction they grew up in and work hard at building a beautiful life for themselves and their children. Others spiral downward and end up living with even more dysfunction and drama than their parents. Unfortunately, their children suffer as their needs for guidance and a proper upbringing remain unmet.

If you are the person who has come so far, and you are now reaping the benefits of a healthy and stable family, you naturally want to protect your own children from the influences of others who aren't making wise decisions. This may include some of your extended family members. If this is the case, don't feel guilty about it!

It doesn't mean that you have to be mean or unkind, but it does mean that you have to set clear boundaries with certain people. As you have grown and matured, you have probably noticed that over time, you began to feel less comfortable around the familiar family dysfunction. Although you never liked it, it was familiar.

Many times, families become so different that those on the outside looking in may wonder how you were ever a part of that situation. They may ask, "Are you sure the stork didn't drop you on the doorstep?" I'm not talking about cutting off your extended family, but instead, living your life without being burdened with unfounded guilt—for doing so well when others are not. I know that it is hard to watch children grow up in less than ideal settings, and there may be some ways you can reach out to them. Again, if it becomes a question of exposing your family to undesirable influences, your first responsibility is to your own children. Isaiah 54:13 (NIV) highlights the importance of godly influence in the lives of our children: "All your children will be taught by the Lord, and great will be their peace."

May God give you the strength and courage to let go of guilt and set healthy boundaries with others.

Reflections

1. What irrational guilt do you carry regarding your extended family?

_____

_____

_____

_____

2. Describe how your life is different from your extended family.

_____

_____

_____

_____

3. How far have you come as you rise above the generational dysfunction in your family?

_____

_____

_____

_____

4. What healthy boundaries have you set around your own nuclear family?

_____

_____

_____

_____

Journal Your Thoughts and Feelings

19

Beware of Counterfeits

I can't stress enough the importance of not settling for counterfeits. A common phrase I use in therapy when I am working with women trapped in an abusive or unhealthy relationship is, "You always get what you settle for." On the surface, those words may sound hard-hearted and uncaring, but they are true. We always get what we settle for.

When a woman deals with this type of drama, she ends up missing what God has for her. She settles, wasting her time and energy as her self-esteem diminishes. The intensity of a dysfunctional dating relationship often leads to an emotional addiction that becomes increasingly more powerful over time.

I call this a counterfeit relationship because there is a replacement of mutual love and respect with control and dependency. Even if an appropriate partner shows her interest, she will not notice, or will purposely ignore his attentions to hold on to what she already has. Years later, she may remorsefully look back and realize what she has done.

We often forget how much our heavenly Father loves us and that He desires good things for us. He wants us to wait on His direction and provision and not to settle for counterfeits. His Word is clear about how a woman should be treated by her partner. Colossians 3:19 (NIV) admonishes husbands to "love your wives and do not be harsh with them."

If you are a woman who has grown up in generational dysfunction, it is crucial to be aware of counterfeits. They can disguise themselves as Mr. Wonderful, but over time, most begin to show their true colors. By God's grace, you can overcome the tendency to settle for less than you deserve and learn to love and value yourself enough to choose a partner who will treat you with genuine love and respect.

Reflections

1. In what ways have you settled for less than what God desires for your life?

_____

_____

_____

_____

2. Have you ever been in a dating relationship that was counterfeit? If so, explain.

_____

_____

_____

_____

3. How has this type of relationship affected your self-esteem?

_____

_____

_____

_____

4. If you are dating, make a list of what you want in a healthy relationship.

_____

_____

_____

_____

Journal Your Thoughts and Feelings

_____

_____

_____

_____

_____

_____

_____

_____

_____

_____

_____

_____

_____

_____

_____

_____

_____

_____

_____

_____

_____

_____

_____

_____

_____

_____

20

What's Your New Defense?

Throughout my years of practice as a marriage and family therapist, I have discovered that defenses are a big deal. Once people have them in place, they hold on to them tightly, even if those very defenses are sabotaging their lives. You may ask, "Why would they do that?" One reason is that those defenses were necessary for their survival at an earlier time in their lives. Abuse, neglect, or negativity would have emotionally destroyed them if they had not been emotionally armored up during their childhoods. For example, the child of an abusive, angry parent may have learned that it was safer to keep his or her feelings inside. That person now struggles in his or her marriage as a result of not being comfortable with emotional intimacy.

As humans, we all have a strong built-in survival instinct. One of the hardest things to accomplish in therapy is to help people learn to trust enough to relax their defensiveness, or at least to store away certain defenses in a tool chest, only taking them out if realistically needed. For most, this is a more desirable option than asking someone to throw away something so valuable.

God's Word teaches us to armor up, but not against each other. We are to love others and to trust God. It is our spiritual enemy, the devil, whom we are to stand up against as we put on the full armor of God.

> Put on the full armor of God, so that you can take your stand against the devil's schemes. For our struggle is not against flesh and blood, but against the rulers, against the authorities, against the powers of this dark world and against the spiritual forces of evil in the heavenly realms. Therefore put on the full armor of God, so that when the day of evil comes, you may be able to stand your ground, and after you have done everything, to stand. Stand firm then, with the belt of truth buckled around your waist, with the breastplate of righteousness in place, and with your feet fitted with the readiness that comes from the gospel of peace. In addition to all this, take up the shield of faith, with which you can extinguish all the flaming arrows of the evil one. Take the helmet of salvation and the sword of the Spirit, which is the word of God. And pray in the Spirit on all occasions with all kinds of prayers and requests. With this in mind, be alert and always keep on praying for all the Lord's people. (Ephesians 6:11–17 NIV)

Reflections

1. Identify some of your defense mechanisms.

_____

_____

_____

_____

2. How are your defenses sabotaging your relationships?

_____

_____

_____

_____

3. Which defenses are you willing to let go of?

_____

_____

_____

_____

_____

4. Are there any defenses that you want to put away in your toolbox?

_____

_____

_____

_____

Journal Your Thoughts and Feelings

For the Spirit God gave us does not make us timid, but gives us power, love, and self-discipline.

—2 Timothy 1:7 (NIV)

21

Discipline and Tenacity of Purpose

Discipline is to train ourselves in the exercise of self-control. Tenacity is the quality of being very determined and persistent. Purpose is one's intention or goal.

On the road to leaving our generational dysfunction behind us, we will have to draw upon discipline and tenacity of purpose to keep us going in the right direction. The pull of generational dysfunction rears its ugly head at the most inopportune times—when we are tired, stressed, or even just hungry.

I remember when, as a young mother, I persistently pursued my purpose of earning my college degree. It wasn't easy with two small children, a husband, and a home. Yet I was very determined to reach my goal. It had meaning to me. It was important! Although it took a little longer, discipline and tenacity paid off. I have never regretted that time in my life. The extra effort during those early years laid the foundation for further education and a professional career.

No one else in my family had graduated from college, except a cousin who had become a medical doctor. I wanted to break this pattern and pass a new standard down to my children. Now, years later, my children have benefited from my choices and enjoy their own successful professional careers as a result of their discipline and tenacity of purpose. There is no question about college for the grandchildren—of course they will go. An old generational pattern has been replaced with a new one.

Over the years in my counseling practice, I have seen others who have shown great self-discipline and tenacity of purpose as they worked to break negative patterns in their own lives. One young woman, whose parents had both died young from health issues, decided she wanted something better for her life. It was exciting to watch as she took control of her health by changing her dietary and exercise habits. She realized that she did not have to be a victim of behaviors she had learned from her parents. Instead of doing what was familiar, she drew upon her inner strength to make better choices.

Another example is a young man who wanted to change the relationship dynamic that he had experienced with his father while growing up. Having been raised by an unavailable father himself, his dad had spent most of his time working and very little time getting to know his son. To break this generational pattern, the young father of three boys began scheduling individual time with each of his sons. At times this was not very easy to work into his busy schedule, but because it was important to him, he made it a priority.

Colossians 3:23 (NIV) tells us, "Whatever you do, work

at it with all your heart, as working for the Lord, not for human masters." We will have numerous opportunities throughout our lives to practice discipline and tenacity of purpose. Our confidence grows as we look back on past successes that reassure us we can again move forward. We don't have to get stuck in the mire!

Reflections

1. In what areas of your life are you exercising discipline?

   _____

   _____

   _____

   _____

2. What are your most undisciplined habits?

   _____

   _____

   _____

   _____

3. Where does tenacity of purpose show up most in your life?

   _____

   _____

   _____

   _____

4. What negative patterns in your life have required the greatest level of discipline and tenacity of purpose to overcome?

   _____

   _____

   _____

   _____

Journal Your Thoughts and Feelings

_____

_____

_____

_____

_____

_____

_____

_____

_____

_____

_____

_____

_____

_____

_____

_____

_____

_____

_____

_____

_____

_____

_____

_____

_____

22

What about Change?

Change finds all of us at different times in our lives, but it seems the most poignant during the holidays. For those who have lost a loved one, the sting of grief and loneliness hits hard during this time. Family traditions that may have been in place for years change in the absence of a spouse or family member.

I have experienced this change in my own life and understand the loss of equilibrium that takes place. Although you try to preserve some of your family traditions for the sake of stability, it's not the same. So you muddle through, secretly wishing the festivities were over.

Traditions add structure and continuity to our lives. They give us a sense of stability and security amid life's ups and downs, but when radical change hits—a change that can't be ignored or denied—we feel the impact. Everything seems amiss, and we are left hobbling on one leg, so to speak, until we can find our balance again.

Yet with God's grace and strength, we do find our balance

again. We learn to trust Him with our future and with our present. Although our holiday traditions will never be the same, we find ways to integrate their sense of purpose into our new celebrations. We learn to appreciate those around us even more as we create new memories with family and friends.

Isaiah 26:3–4 (NIV) tells us, "You will keep in perfect peace those whose minds are steadfast, because they trust in you. Trust in the Lord forever, for the Lord, the Lord himself, is the Rock Eternal." May God bless you if this holiday season finds you in the midst of change you didn't ask for or change you didn't expect. May the comfort of the Holy Spirit flow over you like a warm, soothing balm, and may God's unfailing love give you the stability and strength your heart desires.

Reflections

1. Describe a recent or past loss or change that has affected your life.

_____

_____

_____

_____

2. How did you react to the change?

_____

_____

_____

_____

3. Have you found the holidays to trigger sadness about a loss in your life? If so, in what way?

_____

_____

_____

_____

4. What new holiday traditions have brought a sense of stability back into your life?

_____

_____

_____

_____

Journal Your Thoughts and Feelings

To every *thing there is* a season, and a time to every purpose under the heaven.

—Ecclesiastes 3:1 (KJV)

23

Life-Stage Reevaluation

If you're like me, you may be wondering whether it's time for a life-stage reevaluation. I recently spoke with a longtime friend and realized that she had some of the same thoughts that were going through my mind. We were both acutely aware that as a natural progression of children and grandchildren growing up, our role in the family has changed. We both admitted that this change has seemingly taken us by surprise, along with some not so comfortable feelings. A life-stage reevaluation seemed in order. As I began to identify areas of change that were up for reevaluation, priorities, goals, expectations, lifestyle, self-concept, and a sense of purpose were at the top of my list.

It is normal and healthy for our priorities to shift throughout our lives. At this stage, I realize that my relationship with God is a continuing priority on an even deeper level, based on years of experiencing His love and faithfulness. This stage of life is a time in life to enjoy my relationship with my husband and the comfort of family and trusted friends.

This reevaluation of my goals brings me to realize that they are more present—not years or decades away. They include health and fitness and pursuing writing projects, as well as simply relaxing and enjoying life. I now have the opportunity to enjoy travel, hobbies, and even some self-indulgence and pampering. And yes, without guilt! Most of us have worked hard for many years, raised children, and run a household. A gentler pace is perfectly acceptable now.

As far as expectations go, I am understanding more and more that we can't base our happiness on the behaviors of others. It is better to let them be who they are and not have any preconceived expectations of how they should "bless" our lives. Instead, discover the greater joy of focusing more on how you can be a blessing to someone else.

Then there is the matter of self-concept and a sense of purpose. Along with changing roles as we age, retirement can seemingly leave a void. It's best not to get stuck there. Reevaluate! Base your self-concept on how God sees you, not on what you imagine others think or say about you. You are a product of your life experiences and what you have learned from them. This experience adds texture and richness to your life and forms your character.

Find a new purpose as you pursue opportunities to make a difference in the world and the lives of others. I see great purpose in being loving and supportive of my husband, children, and grandchildren. I still find fulfillment in using the gifts God has given me to listen to others as they struggle with difficulties in their lives. Often, it is the small, behind-the-scenes encouragement that has the most significant impact.

If you are trying to rigidly hold on to an outdated life stage that doesn't seem to fit anymore, I want to encourage you to do your own life-stage reevaluation and start enjoying your life again!

Reflections

1. Are you rigidly trying to hold on to an outdated life stage that doesn't fit anymore? If so, explain.

_____

_____

_____

_____

2. How have your priorities shifted throughout your life?

_____

_____

_____

_____

3. Are your expectations of others bringing you joy or disappointment? Explain.

_____

_____

_____

_____

4. In what ways are you a product of your life experiences, and what you have learned from them?

_____

_____

_____

_____

Journal Your Thoughts and Feelings

_____

_____

_____

_____

_____

_____

_____

_____

_____

_____

_____

_____

_____

_____

_____

_____

_____

_____

_____

_____

_____

_____

_____

_____

_____

_____

_____

_____

24

Feeling Manipulated?

If you've ever felt manipulated, there was most likely a controller in the mix. Controllers are those who want to be in charge not just of their own lives but also of yours. All the while, controllers proclaim that they are "just trying to help," but sometimes "help" is the sunny side of control. The best way to discern whether people's help has crossed over into control is just that. Have they crossed your boundaries? Are you feeling put down, as though they know your mind better than you? Are you feeling uncomfortable or even angry?

Don't negate your feelings. God gave us the capacity to feel for a reason, often to protect us from danger. The stove is hot, and we pull away to protect our skin from being burned. Our emotions serve the same purpose—a warning signal that something is wrong.

Galatians 1:10 (NIV) says, "Am I now trying to win the approval of human beings, or of God? Or am I trying to please people?" It is not emotionally healthy for you to allow yourself to be manipulated or controlled by another person who needs to feel superior or who is not aware of his or her hidden motives. You can handle this type of situation by speaking the truth in love. Kindly take action to preserve your dignity and self-respect. Set clear boundaries in relationships and stay healthy!

Reflections

1. Do you have a controller in your life? Explain.

_____

_____

_____

_____

2. Describe an incident when you felt manipulated, or when you were the manipulator.

_____

_____

_____

_____

3. Are you a people pleaser? If so, how can this become unhealthy for you?

_____

_____

_____

_____

4. What boundaries do you need to set in your relationships to stay healthy?

_____

_____

_____

_____

Journal Your Thoughts and Feelings

_____

_____

_____

_____

_____

_____

_____

_____

_____

_____

_____

_____

_____

_____

_____

_____

_____

_____

_____

_____

_____

_____

_____

_____

_____

_____

Fear not, for I am with you; be not dismayed, for I am your God; I will strengthen you, I will help you, I will uphold you with my righteous right hand.

—Isaiah 41:10 (ESV)

25

Take Time to Grieve

We all experience loss in one form or another during our lives, and it may be tempting to repress feelings of grief. After all, you need to get on with your life, right? Wrong! I can't stress enough how important it is for you to take the time to grieve.

If you ignore, stuff, or deny your feelings, they will come to the surface in one situation or another—sometimes years down the road. Our feelings of sadness and grief can overwhelm and frighten us. We aren't used to this level of intensity, and most of us are uncomfortable with it. For example, some people avoid crying after a loss because they're afraid that once they start, they won't be able to stop. Yet those tears are cathartic, a healing balm. Others grew up in homes where the implicit message was to not talk about feelings.

God promises to be with us when we are walking through grief. Psalm 34:18 (NIV) tells us, "The Lord is close to the broken-hearted and saves those who are crushed in spirit." He has graciously given us the comfort of His Holy Spirit, but we can only receive encouragement when we acknowledge our pain. You can break the dysfunctional pattern of repressing your feelings, knowing that God is with you and He sees your hurts. He has not left you comfortless.

Reflections

1. What did you learn from your parents or grandparents about how to deal with feelings?

   _____

   _____

   _____

   _____

2. Do you repress your feelings at times? If so, give an example.

   _____

   _____

   _____

   _____

3. Have you experienced a loss that you have not fully grieved? Explain.

   _____

   _____

   _____

   _____

4. How can you draw upon God's comfort and grace to break the dysfunctional pattern of repressing your feelings?

   _____

   _____

   _____

   _____

Journal Your Thoughts and Feelings

_____

_____

_____

_____

_____

_____

_____

_____

_____

_____

_____

_____

_____

_____

_____

_____

_____

_____

_____

_____

_____

_____

_____

_____

_____

_____

_____

_____

26

Don't Let Your Problems Impress You

In therapy, we often hear the phrase "get in touch with your feelings," and this is an essential aspect of good mental health. Don't deny or repress your feelings. Yet there is a time to put things into perspective rationally. In other words, don't give your problems so much power or attention that they overwhelm you and cause you to lose sight of the greatness of God. He is bigger than all our problems. He is our big God, our God who can do anything. Psalm 50:15 (NAB) tells us to "Call upon me in the day of trouble; I will rescue you, and you will honor me."

I have watched my counseling clients gain emotional freedom as they grasp the concept that it is not the situation that produces troublesome feelings, but what we tell ourselves about the situation. They experience greater peace and stability when they cease being at the mercy of external circumstances. Empowered to choose their thoughts and responses rather than reacting, they can step off of the drama roller coaster and focus more clearly on the positive aspects of their lives.

I have a good friend who has had many physical problems over the years. Yet she often says, "It's just a bump in the road." Some of those bumps in the road have looked pretty serious to me. How does she do it? She calls on God, trusts Him to help her, and then gets right back to her focus of honoring Him in her life. She doesn't let her problems impress her!

My friend keeps on going with a smile on her face and praise in her heart. She is an excellent example for all of us as we learn the value of not letting our problems impress us.

Reflections

1. What problems in your life have you allowed to overwhelm you and drain your energy?

_____

_____

_____

_____

2. What are you telling yourself about these problems?

_____

_____

_____

_____

3. What feelings are you experiencing as a result of your thoughts about these problems?

_____

_____

_____

_____

4. What steps can you take to begin to choose your thoughts and responses rather than reacting to circumstances?

_____

_____

_____

_____

Journal Your Thoughts and Feelings

27

Distracted

Generational patterns of fragmentation and instability can run deep in families—divorce, relationship difficulties, emotional cutoff, or chronic job changes. With that in mind, it is no wonder individuals find themselves sabotaging their lives and success by allowing themselves to get distracted and unfocused.

Have you ever had times in your life when one distraction after another seemed to get you off track? Maybe it was during your workday when you had a deadline to meet, and the phone rings ten times, or a coworker drops by to ask a few questions. You know what I mean, right? After each distraction, it becomes more difficult to refocus on what you were initially trying to accomplish.

These distractions can be large or small. Sometimes the small ones do the most damage because we don't readily recognize them as troublesome—until we experience their cumulative effect. This type of distraction can take the form of people grumbling or being judgmental at work or in your social circle. Although it is easy to overlook early on, over time, you may begin to feel undermined and start doubting yourself.

More substantial distractions can include health issues, relationship problems, or financial difficulties. You may ask, "How do I stay focused on what God has called me to do or on the goals I have for my life?" God's Word gives us the answer: "Let your eyes look straight ahead; fix your gaze directly before you. Give careful thought to the paths for your feet and be steadfast in all your ways." (Proverbs 4:25–26 NIV). In other words, don't get distracted!

Reflections

1. What generational patterns of instability have you observed in your family of origin?

_____

_____

_____

_____

2. How have these dysfunctional patterns affected your own life?

_____

_____

_____

_____

3. What distractions have you allowed to get you off track?

_____

_____

_____

_____

4. Name the small distractions that are having a cumulative effect on your life?

_____

_____

_____

_____

Journal Your Thoughts and Feelings

_____

_____

_____

_____

_____

_____

_____

_____

_____

_____

_____

_____

_____

_____

_____

_____

_____

_____

_____

_____

_____

_____

_____

_____

_____

_____

_____

_____

Whoever is kind to the poor lends to the Lord, and he will reward them for what they have done.

—Proverbs 19:17 (NIV)

28

People Helping People

In dysfunctional circles, help can be the sunny side of control, but I'm not talking about this kind of help. You will know what I'm talking about if you have ever spent a day at Mayo Clinic. My husband and I recently spent most of the day there in between several scheduled appointments. Our itinerary allowed us enough time to mosey down to the cafeteria and make a few trips on the elevator.

We found this environment to be completely different than what we experience on a day-to-day basis, so of course it stood out to me. We were in the orthopedic area, and I observed people in wheelchairs or walking with canes, some with bandaged limbs. That in itself was not what caught my attention—it was people helping people. Everywhere I looked, someone was helping someone—an adult son pushing a father along in his wheelchair, or an older man lovingly and patiently holding his wife's arm as she strolled from the cafeteria.

God's Word tells us to carry each other's burdens, to help

each other. In doing this, we are fulfilling the law of Christ, which is the law of love. "Carry each other's burdens and in this way you will fulfill the law of Christ." (Galatians 6:2 NASB).

May our eyes be open to those around us who are carrying heavy burdens. Their needs may not be as apparent as the person in the wheelchair. It may be an inner hurt, a heavy heart, or a broken spirit. Maybe a kind word or a smile from you will be enough to brighten their day!

Reflections

1. What is the difference between help and control?

    _____

    _____

    _____

    _____

2. What did you observe in your family of origin concerning this issue?

    _____

    _____

    _____

    _____

3. What does Jesus teach us about helping others?

    _____

    _____

    _____

    _____

4. How did you feel when someone came along beside you to help you during a difficult time in your life?

    _____

    _____

    _____

    _____

Journal Your Thoughts and Feelings

29

Mercy—Seeing, Feeling,
and Taking Action

One of the best ways to overcome patterns of generational dysfunction is to realize that everything isn't about us. We must learn to be merciful to others. Mercy is seeing someone's need, having empathy and compassion for that person, and taking the time to help. Sometimes we stop with the seeing and walk on by in our busy lives. Other times we go a step further and actually feel compassion for the person, maybe even pray for them—and then go on with our busy schedule. But true mercy takes action to meet the person's need.

You may say, "I can't fully meet the person's need. It is too big for me. I don't have the resources for that." You may be right. It may be more than you can individually provide. But ask yourself, "What *can* I do? Could I make a difference in some way in this person's life?" Remember the little boy with the two fish and five loaves of bread? He gave what he had, and God blessed it, stretched it, and made it sufficient for the need.

The Bible teaches us to show mercy. Micah 6:8 (NIV) tells us, "He has shown you, O mortal, what is good. And what does the Lord require of you? To act justly and to love mercy and to walk humbly with your God." Proverbs 3:3–4 (KJV) says, "Let not mercy and truth forsake thee: bind them about thy neck; write them upon the table of thine heart: So shalt thou find favor and good understanding in the sight of God and man."

In fact, in Matthew 25:34–40 (NIV), we can see that Jesus takes our behavior toward others *very* personally.

> Then the King will say to those on his right, "Come, you who are blessed by my Father, take your inheritance, the kingdom prepared for you since the creation of the world. For I was hungry and you gave me something to eat, I was thirsty and you gave me something to drink, I was a stranger and you invited me in, I needed clothes and you clothed me, I was sick and you looked after me, I was in prison and you came to visit me." Then the righteous will answer him, "Lord, when did we see you hungry and feed you, or thirsty and give you something to drink? When did we see you a stranger and invite you in, or needing clothes and clothe you? When did we see you sick or in prison and go to visit you?" The King will reply, "Truly I tell you, whatever you did for one of the least of these brothers and sisters of mine, you did for me." He will reply, "Truly

I tell you, whatever you did not do for one of
the least of these, you did not do for me."

Don't excuse yourself from showing mercy to others just
because you have had difficulties in life. Don't make the
mistake of assuming you have nothing to give. Reaching out
to others who are in need will allow God's healing love to
flow through you to them. Don't let your past keep you from
the beautiful experience of showing mercy to others today.

Reflections

1. What is true mercy?

_____

_____

_____

2. Give an example of a time when you showed mercy to another person.

_____

_____

_____

3. Give an example of a situation where you felt mercy for someone but did not act on your feeling because you believed the need was too great for you to make a difference.

_____

_____

_____

4. Have you assumed that you have nothing to give because of your past struggles in life? If so, what steps can you take today to allow God's healing love and grace to flow through you to others?

_____

_____

_____

_____

Journal Your Thoughts and Feelings

Judge not, and ye shall not be judged: condemn not, and ye shall not be condemned: forgive, and ye shall be forgiven.

—Luke 6:37 (KJV)

30

Love Covers a Multitude of Sins

> But the end of all things is at hand: be ye therefore sober, and watch unto prayer. And above all things have fervent charity amongst yourselves: for charity shall cover the multitude of sins.
>
> —1 Peter 4:7–8 (KJV)

As I listened to a sermon on getting prepared for end-times, I was surprised at the emphasis of the message. The minister wasn't telling us where to put our money or to store up food in preparation for hard times. Instead, he told us to prepare our hearts so that we did not hinder the work of the Holy Spirit in the end-time, during the "latter rains before the harvest." "Be patient therefore, brethren, unto the coming of the Lord. Behold, the husbandman waiteth for the precious fruit of the earth, and hath long patience for it, until he receive the former and latter rain." (James 5:7 KJV).

Because scripture tells us, as believers, to have fervent charity (love) among ourselves, not only are we to forgive anyone who has hurt us, but also we are to cover their offense. That's the part that stood out to me. I had never heard it said quite like this before. I can't cover someone's sin against God, but I can cover someone's sin against me. In other words, I can choose to not talk about it to others, not spread it around, and not keep bringing it up ten or twenty years later. It also means that I ask God to remove any root of bitterness that is in my heart.

This is radical Christianity in its purest form. It is grace, and yes, it goes entirely against the grain of our human nature. We say we have forgiven someone because as Christians, we know that because God has forgiven us, it is what we're supposed to do. But how many of us find ourselves bringing up the matter to friends and family on more than one occasion? Somehow we rationalize that it's okay because, after all, don't we need a little support and understanding from those who care about us? A little sympathy or prayer?

As a therapist, I'm used to people bringing their problems to me in confidence, but I am doing them a disservice if I don't lead them in the direction of forgiveness and letting go of bitterness. Empathy and advice from a trusted friend and confidant can be healing and valuable when it doesn't become a substitute for taking the situation to God and acting in love.

James 5:8–9 (KJV) tells us, "Be ye also patient; stablish your hearts: for the coming of the Lord draweth nigh. Grudge not one another, brethren, lest ye be condemned: behold, the judge standeth before the door." These verses make it evident that how we treat each other is linked to our preparation for the coming of the Lord. It may seem unfair that the person who has been hurt by another is left with the burden of forgiving and covering that person's offense. Yet this is what we are admonished to do.

It is for our own good to forgive and release any root of bitterness before it has time to grow. It doesn't mean that we delude ourselves into thinking that the other person's behavior was right. It doesn't mean that we always stay in the path of a hurtful person, but it does mean that we forgive and even pray for them. One of the best ways to get rid of resentment is to pray for people when a negative emotion or thought about them flashes through your mind. It is also important to remember that God can use a negative situation for our good as He prepares us for eternity.

Reflections

1. How is covering someone's offense toward you different than being in denial?

_____

_____

_____

_____

2. How is covering someone's offense toward you different than just stuffing your feelings?

_____

_____

_____

_____

3. In what ways can you extend grace to someone who has offended you?

_____

_____

_____

_____

4. How can you apply James 5:8–9 to your own life?

_____

_____

_____

_____

Journal Your Thoughts and Feelings

_____

_____

_____

_____

_____

_____

_____

_____

_____

_____

_____

_____

_____

_____

_____

_____

_____

_____

_____

_____

_____

_____

_____

_____

_____

31

A Higher Standard

If you love those who love you, what credit is
that to you? Even sinners love those who love
them. And if you do good to those who are
good to you, what credit is that to you? Even
sinners do that. And if you lend to those from
whom you expect payment, what credit is that
to you? Even sinners lend to sinners, expecting
to be repaid in full. But love your enemies,
do good to them, and lend to them without
expecting to get anything back. Then your
reward will be great, and you will be children
of the Most High because He is kind to the
ungrateful and wicked. Be merciful, just as
your Father is merciful.

—Luke 6:32—36 (NIV)

Do you struggle to live up to this high standard? Jesus's
words speak volumes in this passage of scripture. It isn't

merely a standard of behavior purported by a theologian or teacher. It is God's standard for us as His children.

He knows we're not perfect, just as we know our children will mess up and fall short of what we expect of them. That doesn't keep us from setting a high standard of behavior for them because we are aware that they are watching our example. Our heavenly Father gives us His example to follow. He is kind and merciful to the ungrateful and wicked.

I don't know about you, but when I'm honest with myself, my natural tendency is to think negative thoughts about people who haven't necessarily been good to me, my family, or my friends. I rationalize this by mentally judging their behaviors and feeling justified in my assessment. Yet Jesus calls us to a higher standard.

May each of us reach toward the goal God has set for us as believers. Of course, we can't do this in the flesh, but we can have the fruit of the Spirit in our lives as we walk in the Spirit. John 15:4 (NASB) admonishes us, "Abide in Me, and I in you. As the branch cannot bear fruit of itself unless it abides in the vine, so neither can you unless you abide in Me." When we abide in Christ, He empowers us as we endeavor to be more like Him.

Reflections

1. What is God's standard for loving others?

_____

_____

_____

_____

2. In what ways do you struggle to live up to this high standard?

_____

_____

_____

_____

3. What is your natural tendency toward those who display negative behaviors toward you?

_____

_____

_____

_____

4. What rationalizations do you use to justify your reactions?

_____

_____

_____

_____

Journal Your Thoughts and Feelings

_____

_____

_____

_____

_____

_____

_____

_____

_____

_____

_____

_____

_____

_____

_____

_____

_____

_____

_____

_____

_____

_____

_____

_____

_____

_____

_____

_____

_____

32

Just Love Everyone

The words on a church sign caught my eye as I was driving home one day. "Just love everyone, and I'll take care of everything else later." As I reflected on the meaning, it began to make sense. Christ's admonition to His followers is to "love one another" and to "judge not."

We all have difficult people in our lives—or maybe *we* are the difficult person in someone else's life without even realizing it. We all have our blind spots. Holidays or special events have a way of bringing us together with family, friends, and coworkers. We may not be used to spending much time with some of these people, and it's more than likely that we will find ourselves passing judgment (if not verbally, then in our minds) about some of them. Then we ration our love, kindness, or attention based on our assessment, which may or may not be accurate. We might forget to make allowance for the growth and change cousin Joe has undergone since his last escapade hit the gossip mill.

As I thought more about the words on the church sign,

I was reminded that Christ loved us when we were lost and undone. He didn't just love us enough to be polite and cordial—He loved us enough to come down to earth and die for our sins. If He can love me that much, then shouldn't I, in turn, love others rather than judge them? I have no idea what He has in store for their lives or how He is reaching out to them. Who knows? Perhaps my loving behavior toward someone is part of His plan to draw that person closer to Him.

John 13:34 (NIV) says, "A new command I give you: Love one another. As I have loved you, so you must love one another." So going forward, why don't we purpose in our hearts to just love everyone and let Him take care of the rest?

Reflections

1. Identify the difficult people in your life.

_____

_____

_____

_____

2. Could it be possible that *you* are the difficult person in someone else's life?

_____

_____

_____

_____

3. In what ways are you prone to judging others?

_____

_____

_____

_____

4. Are you aware of any behaviors or attitudes that may be coming across as unloving to others? If so, be specific and honest with yourself.

_____

_____

_____

_____

Journal Your Thoughts and Feelings

Draw near to God and He will draw near to you.

—James 4:8 (NASB)

33

Forget Not Our Closeness

When you are tempted, I admonish you to count the cost. Adam and Eve had no idea of what their disobedience would cost—their closeness with God. They had enjoyed walking and talking with Him in the Garden of Eden. After sinning, they hid from His presence. Being deceived, they traded their closeness with their Creator for the instant gratification of their desires.

I knew a young, beautiful woman who compromised her values. After having lost her marriage as a result of her husband's infidelity, she was the most vulnerable she had ever been in her life—lonely, feeling unloved, and cast aside.

As we talked, it was evident she was hiding from her heavenly Father. Rather than seeking comfort and strength in His presence, she had accepted Satan's counterfeit. I tried to help her see that her desires for love and companionship were understandable, but the path she had chosen came with too great of a price: her closeness with God. You see, Satan is not trying to give us satisfaction and pleasure when he tempts us to sin—he is trying to separate us from God. James 4:7–8 (NIV) tells us to "Submit therefore to God. Resist the devil and he will flee from you. Draw near to God and He will draw near to you."

God's Word tells us to guard our hearts. "Do not love the world or the things in the world. If anyone loves the world, the love of the Father is not in him. For all that is in the world—the desires of the flesh and the desires of the eyes and pride in possessions—is not from the Father but is from the world. And the world is passing away along with its desires, but whoever does the will of God abides forever." (1 John 2:15—17 ESV).

Our heavenly Father desires a close relationship with us. Through Christ, He has provided a way to restore our relationship with Him. "If we confess our sins, he is faithful and just to forgive us our sins, and to cleanse us from all unrighteousness." (1 John 1:9 KJV). Don't let your sense of failure and shame keep you from running back into His outstretched arms.

Reflections

1. Describe what it means to have a close relationship with God?

_____

_____

_____

_____

2. Has there been a time in your life when you felt you were not as close to God as you had been previously? Explain.

_____

_____

_____

_____

3. Is there anything or anyone you value more than your closeness with God?

_____

_____

_____

_____

4. How would you describe the deceptiveness of temptation?

_____

_____

_____

_____

Journal Your Thoughts and Feelings

_____

_____

_____

_____

_____

_____

_____

_____

_____

_____

_____

_____

_____

_____

_____

_____

_____

_____

_____

_____

_____

_____

_____

_____

_____

_____

_____

_____

34

Praying and Singing

Is anyone among you in trouble? Let them pray. Is anyone happy? Let them sing songs of praise.

—James 5:13 (NIV)

Praying and singing our way through life seems to be what we are encouraged to do. We are not exempt from hardships, but we know what to do during those trying times: pray! In contrast, if we are happy, we should sing praises to God.

Let's take a look at what sometimes takes place instead. If you are suffering hardship, do you pray, or do you complain? Maybe you pray *and* complain. When you are happy, do you sing praises, or do you take your comfortable position for granted, neither praying nor singing?

God's Word gives us direction on how to handle the ups and downs of life without becoming overwhelmed, feeling overly stressed, or losing our peace. It is human nature to complain and to take our blessings for granted, but in Christ, our spiritual man seeks to draw closer to God during times of adversity and during times of blessing.

It doesn't have to be one or the other as we learn that our peace comes from His presence and not from perfect circumstances. This trust is the secret to stability in our lives. I hope you will draw strength from your closeness to God, regardless of the circumstances. May you keep on praying and singing!

Reflections

1. How do you handle hardships and difficult circumstances?

_____

_____

_____

_____

2. Describe a situation that has caused you to feel overwhelmed and stressed.

_____

_____

_____

_____

3. In what way has prayer been a source of comfort to you during times of difficulty?

_____

_____

_____

_____

_____

4. How did your parents express joy and happiness?

_____

_____

_____

_____

Journal Your Thoughts and Feelings

_____

_____

_____

_____

_____

_____

_____

_____

_____

_____

_____

_____

_____

_____

_____

_____

_____

_____

_____

_____

_____

_____

_____

_____

35

When God Shows Up

Have you ever experienced a situation where you were in over your head, couldn't see your way clear, and faced resistance on every hand? Then God showed up, and you knew deep in your soul that it wasn't just a coincidence—it was a God thing.

I have experienced this numerous times in my life, and I experienced it again recently. I texted my close friend, "Oh my, we just experienced a God thing," as I proceeded to tell her the details of God's intervention. It was so clear, so relevant to our needs, that it couldn't be confused with a mere chance. My husband and I were in awe at the preciseness of God's care in meeting the need at hand.

Earlier in the day, I had read about seeking God's purposes rather than pursuing our own plans. We plan so many things in our daily lives, but it is God who controls the outcome. God's Word tells us, "Come now you who say, 'Today or tomorrow we will go to such a city, and spend a year there and engage in business and make a profit.' You do not know what your life will be like tomorrow. You are just a vapor that appears for a little while and then vanishes away. Instead, you ought to say, 'If the Lord wills, we will live and also do this or that.' But as it is, you boast in your arrogance; all such boasting is evil." (James 4:13–16 NASB).

Sometimes we plan God right out of our lives without giving Him room to interrupt our plans. But as we come to the end of ourselves and invite Him to be a part of the process, He shows up, and we receive the blessing of His active and loving participation in our lives!

Reflections

1. Discuss a situation where you felt overwhelmed and lacking in resources.

   _____

   _____

   _____

   _____

2. Have you ever experienced a God thing? Describe.

   _____

   _____

   _____

   _____

3. In what ways do you overplan your life?

   _____

   _____

   _____

   _____

4. Do you give God room to interrupt your plans? Explain.

   _____

   _____

   _____

   _____

Journal Your Thoughts and Feelings

The Lord has made everything for its own purpose,

—Proverbs 16:4 (NASB)

36

Purpose

Purpose comes in many forms—family, service, ministry, or career. It's as individual as we are. Yet as we mature and experience life, we are given repeated chances to learn that it isn't about us, that we acquire satisfaction and purpose by participating in God's love for others.

I recently read a passage written by Tony Snow several years ago, before he lost his battle with cancer. Tony shared his heart about what sickness had taught him. I found myself moved by his description of finding true purpose and fulfillment in life by sharing in God's love for others.

I began to think about this in my daily life and my interactions with others. As I became more aware of participating in God's love for others, I was intentional about doing small acts of kindness in the present moment. As a result, I felt a new sense of purpose.

You see, our love isn't perfect. But God's is! We get self-absorbed as we go about our day. It's not that we're trying to be unloving, but we get busy and preoccupied with life's trivial matters. Tony's illness offered him the opportunity to shift his attention from the things that don't matter to the things that do.

When we think of God's abundant and lavish love for us, it is exciting to realize that we can participate in that kind of love. Jesus tells us, "You shall love the Lord your God with all your heart, and with all your soul, and with all your mind." This is the first and great commandment. And the second is like unto it, Thou shalt love thy neighbor as thyself." (Matthew 22:37–39 NASB). As we allow the Holy Spirit to guide us, we can walk in love. It is our privilege to be a part of something greater than ourselves.

May God bless each of us as we find true satisfaction and purpose in participating in His love for others!

Reflections

1. What has given you a sense of purpose in life?

_____

_____

_____

_____

2. In what ways have you found purpose in participating in God's love for others?

_____

_____

_____

_____

3. What experiences in your life have helped you shift your focus from things that don't matter to things that do?

_____

_____

_____

_____

4. List specific daily acts of kindness that you have done that gave you a sense of satisfaction and purpose.

_____

_____

_____

_____

Journal Your Thoughts and Feelings

_____

_____

_____

_____

_____

_____

_____

_____

_____

_____

_____

_____

_____

_____

_____

_____

_____

_____

_____

_____

_____

_____

_____

_____

_____

_____

_____

_____

37

You Are Special

"Know you are My child, My special child, and I love you with a love you cannot understand." As I read the words scribbled on a sheet of paper, I thought about their meaning. A friend had written them down as she felt moved to share them with me. Having been fatherless in the true sense of the word, I didn't really have a good foundation for my understanding of my heavenly Father's love for me. I didn't know how special I was to Him.

Over the years, I have found comfort in knowing that because of Christ, I can have a special relationship with my heavenly Father. It isn't that I am more special than you, but I am important to Him—and so are you! My relationship with Him is special—and so is yours!

You may not have felt loved or valued by your earthly father, but it doesn't matter. That doesn't mean you're not special. The sooner you realize this and begin living your life from that premise, the happier you will be. God's grace is sufficient to fill in the gaps that generational dysfunction left in your life. He is enough, and His love is enough to make up for any failures of an earthly father. In Luke 12:6–7 (NIV), Jesus tells us, "Are not five sparrows sold for two cents? Yet not one of them is forgotten before God. Indeed, the very hairs of your head are all numbered. Do not fear; you are more valuable than many sparrows."

If your childhood experiences have left you feeling insignificant, I encourage you to bask in the love of your heavenly Father and realize just how precious you are to Him.

Reflections

1. Have your childhood experiences left you feeling less than special? If so, in what way?

_____

_____

_____

_____

2. As an adult, have you been able to rise above those experiences? Explain.

_____

_____

_____

_____

3. How has God's grace filled in the gaps that generational dysfunction may have left in your life?

_____

_____

_____

_____

4. List some ways you can learn to bask in the love of your heavenly Father.

_____

_____

_____

_____

Journal Your Thoughts and Feelings

_____

_____

_____

_____

_____

_____

_____

_____

_____

_____

_____

_____

_____

_____

_____

_____

_____

_____

_____

_____

_____

_____

_____

_____

_____

_____

_____

_____

The Lord thy God in the midst of thee *is* mighty; he will save, he will rejoice over thee with joy; he will rest in his love, he will joy over thee with singing.

—Zephaniah 3:17 (KJV)

38

You're Enough

You will struggle with relationships until you get to the place of believing that you are enough. Women will continue to stay in abusive relationships until they know in their heart of hearts that they are enough with or without a man in their lives. I have counseled women who could not bring themselves to separate from an abusive partner, even if they were enduring physical abuse. They kept going back for more until they didn't have enough self-esteem left to walk out the door.

It is sad for a woman to allow herself to be destroyed. It is even worse to see innocent children affected by this type of situation. Grown children often talk about how their mother couldn't seem to leave no matter how bad things were because she was never able to get to the place of knowing she was enough.

God's Word tells us we are enough. We are of great value to God, wonderfully made, deeply loved, and daughters of the King. Psalm 139:13–16 (NIV) tells us, "For you created my inmost being; you knit me together in my mother's womb. I praise you because I am fearfully and wonderfully made; your works are wonderful, I know that full well. My frame was not hidden from you when I was made in the secret place, when I was woven together in the depths of the earth. Your eyes saw my unformed body; all the days ordained for me were written in your book." In Christ, we no longer have to feel unworthy or focus on our human shortcomings; instead, we have forgiveness and love.

If you are a woman who has not gotten to the place of knowing you are enough, I want to encourage you to dig deep into God's Word and find out just how important you are to your Creator. Only then will you be able to live your life in a way that honors the value God has placed on you.

Reflections

1. Do you believe you are enough? Explain.

_____

_____

_____

_____

2. Has self-esteem been a generational issue in your family? Explain.

_____

_____

_____

_____

3. How has Christ's forgiveness and love affected how you feel about yourself?

_____

_____

_____

_____

4. What does it mean to live your life in a way that honors the value God has placed on you?

_____

_____

_____

_____

Journal Your Thoughts and Feelings

_____

_____

_____

_____

_____

_____

_____

_____

_____

_____

_____

_____

_____

_____

_____

_____

_____

_____

_____

_____

_____

_____

_____

_____

_____

_____

_____

_____

_____

39

Your Special Gifts

God has given each of us unique gifts to share with others. Some of those gifts come in the form of natural talent, whereas others are honed through pain, suffering, or loss. I was impressed with the movie *I Can Only Imagine*. I found it to be a beautiful story of God's redemption and grace. As one woman told the songwriter how much his lyrics had touched her life, she asked how long it had taken him to write "I Can Only Imagine." When he said he wrote it in twenty minutes, she told him it didn't take him twenty minutes but a lifetime. She said she couldn't imagine how much he'd had to go through to give her that gift.

As the story of this man's life unfolded, it was evident that his gift came at a great cost. Having grown up with an alcoholic father, he suffered physical and emotional abuse. He had carried his anger and resentment deep inside for most of his life—until God's grace and forgiveness broke through. Years later, his father sought his forgiveness as well as God's, and both father and son received the grace to let go of the past and move forward in love.

Each of us has gifts that God has given us to share with others. As with the songwriter, these gifts are often a result of adversity. As I look back on my own childhood, I have often wondered why my circumstances were less than ideal. "Why couldn't I have been a minister's daughter or grown up in a family of devout Christians?" Yet I now see that the gifts God entrusted me to share with others would not have been developed in an idyllic childhood. I wouldn't have brought the same depth and understanding to my counseling and writing without experiencing hardships.

The same is true for you. I have friends who have experienced adversity in different ways than I have. I can't give their gifts to others, but they can! You see, there is always purpose in the pain. Romans 8:28 (KJV) tells us, "And we know that all things work together for good to them that love God, to them who are the called according to his purpose." With this in mind, may we learn to not be bitter about the difficult circumstances that come into all our lives in one form or another but instead allow God to use those experiences to make us a blessing to others.

Reflections

1. List your unique God-given gifts.

_____

_____

_____

_____

2. Which of those gifts seem to be natural, and which ones were developed through your life experiences?

_____

_____

_____

_____

_____

3. Describe a gift you admire in one of your friends.

_____

_____

_____

_____

4. In what ways are you sharing your unique gifts with others?

_____

_____

_____

_____

Journal Your Thoughts and Feelings

_____

_____

_____

_____

_____

_____

_____

_____

_____

_____

_____

_____

_____

_____

_____

_____

_____

_____

_____

_____

_____

_____

_____

_____

_____

_____

_____

_____

Therefore if any man *be* in Christ, *he is* a new creature: old things are passed away; behold, all things are become new.
—2 Corinthians 5:17 (KJV)

40

New Beginnings

It has been said that the Christian life is a life of many new beginnings. This message is good news to those of us who have needed an extra measure of grace at times. We stumble, get up, dust ourselves off, and keep going—with God's forgiveness, grace, and the power of the Holy Spirit.

We talk a lot about dysfunction and mistakes in the therapy world, but sometimes we have to face the reality of sin and understand that the gospel has a remedy for that. Because of Christ's sacrificial death and resurrection, sin no longer has power over us. "For sin shall not have dominion over you: for ye are not under the law, but under grace. What then? Shall we sin, because we are not under the law, but under grace? God forbid." (Romans 6:14–15 KJV). Verse 22 goes on to say, "But now being made free from sin, and become servants to God, ye have your fruit unto holiness, and the end everlasting life."

As Christians, we embrace each new beginning as a precious gift from God. We don't take it for granted or flippantly misuse God's grace as a license to sin. "My dear children, I write this to you so that you will not sin. But if anybody does sin, we have an advocate with the Father—Jesus Christ, the Righteous One. He is the atoning sacrifice for our sins, and not only for ours but also for the sins of the whole world." (1 John 2:1–2 NIV).

Reflections

1. What new beginnings have you experienced in your life?

_____

_____

_____

_____

2. How has God's grace empowered you to keep on going after making mistakes in life?

_____

_____

_____

_____

3. How do you define dysfunction, mistakes, and sin?

_____

_____

_____

_____

4. What steps can you take today to embrace God's grace and each new beginning in your life as a precious gift?

_____

_____

_____

_____

Journal Your Thoughts and Feelings

_____

_____

_____

_____

_____

_____

_____

_____

_____

_____

_____

_____

_____

_____

_____

_____

_____

_____

_____

_____

_____

_____

_____

_____

_____

_____

_____

You Can Soar

Because of God's grace, you can soar above the storm clouds of generational dysfunction. Just as an airline pilot knows to rise above tumultuous weather, we have an inner compass that motivates us to do so as well. We can rise higher. We were made to soar!

If you have been living in the shadow of generational issues that are controlling your life, damaging your relationships, and stealing your joy, I want to encourage you to break free! It's time to find a higher altitude.

It starts with change and getting unstuck. Many of us won't change until it is more uncomfortable *not* to change than it is to change. If we keep doing the same thing over and over, we will get the same result. If the airline pilot refuses to rise to a higher altitude during turbulence, the passengers will feel the roughness of the ride. Some may become physically ill, experience anxiety, or even get physically hurt. Calmness is only achievable if the plane rises above the storm.

Because of God's love and grace, you can soar above generational dysfunction and find wholeness and healing through Christ.

Invitation

For God so loved the world, that He gave His
only begotten Son, that whoever believes in
Him shall not perish, but have eternal life.

—John 3:16 (NASB)

Sometimes people don't know what to say to God to begin
a relationship with Him. Would you kindly consider
using this prayer to help you? Simply pray this in your mind
and heart to God right now.

Dear God, I realize that I am a sinner, and I
am very sorry for my sins. Please forgive me.
I now believe that Jesus Christ is Your Son
and that He gave His life as a sacrifice for
me. Please come into my life and be my Lord
and Savior. Thank You for Your love for me.
Amen.

Conclusion

My purpose for writing this book is to give encouragement and hope to those struggling with generational dysfunction. As a therapist for over three decades, I have seen firsthand the devastation that results from unrecognized and unaddressed negative patterns of thought and behavior. Families are torn apart, relationships are damaged, and depression and anxiety run rampant in our society. Could there be a better way? My answer is yes! God's Word offers us the wisdom and direction to overcome our generational dysfunctions. Christ's love and grace, and the power of the Holy Spirit, give us the means to do so.

As a therapist, I have observed that as people begin to become healthier emotionally, they also come to a place of spiritual renewal and faith. In turn, their faith gives them the impetus to continue their emotional and relational healing. Relationships are restored, old hurts are healed, and addictions are broken when people discover they can rise above generational dysfunction.

As a family systems therapist, I always look for generational patterns when I work with my patients. The use of a genogram helps both the therapist and the patient have a better understanding of how strong a particular pattern of thought or behavior becomes as it is passed down from generation to generation. This puts things into perspective for the person who is seeking counseling for a particular issue, such as depression or low self-esteem.

Many people allow themselves to become victims of their generational dysfunctions. They live out their days repeating the mistakes of their parents or grandparents, taking the path that is most familiar to them. They build multifaceted ego defenses that allow them to continue in their dysfunction. Yet there is a better path. It is the path of healing through spirituality and grace.

I have found my personal relationship with Christ to be an integral part my journey through generational dysfunction. My heavenly Father has been faithful to reparent me in the areas where my parents fell short. The Holy Spirit continues to lead me on this journey. My prayer is that you, also, will find God to be a good, good Father as you rise above self-defeating patterns and reach your God-given potential. May God's Word provide the light you need to illuminate your path as you find the courage to rise higher!

About the Author

Stephanie Murphy offers guidance and encouragement for those struggling with the effects of generational dysfunction in their lives. She draws not only on her three decades of experience as a marriage and family therapist but also on her personal experiences. Stephanie shares wisdom from God's Word and from her own Christian faith. She has a master's degree in counseling and is a licensed marriage and family therapist. She is actively involved with her husband in his life's work as a missionary to young people in Europe and Costa Rica.

Stephanie is also the author of *Strong and Courageous: Encouragement for Families Touched by Autism* (WestBow Press, 2017) and *Faith, Hope, Courage, and New Beginnings* (WestBow Press, 2017).

Email Stephanie at stephanieannmurphy@icloud.com

Visit her blog at stephanieannmurphy.com

Visit her author website at stephaniemurphychristiancounseling.com

Printed in the United States
By Bookmasters